# Phenomenal
# AOC

## THE ROOTS AND RISE OF
## ALEXANDRIA OCASIO-CORTEZ

*For the phenomenal forces that are my daughters, Sofia, Isabel, and Esmé.*
—A.A.D.

*Para Sam, Mamá, y Papá.*
—L.L.

Phenomenal AOC: The Roots and Rise of Alexandria Ocasio-Cortez • Text copyright © 2022 by Anika Aldamuy Denise • Illustrations copyright © 2022 by Loris Lora, represented by Heflinreps, Inc. • All rights reserved • Manufactured in Italy • No part of this book may be used or reproduced in any manner whatsoever without written permission except in the case of brief quotations embodied in critical articles and reviews. For information address HarperCollins Children's Books, a division of HarperCollins Publishers, 195 Broadway, New York, NY 10007 • www.harpercollinschildrens.com • Library of Congress Control Number: 2021951686 • ISBN 978-0-06-311374-9 • The artist used scanned textures and Adobe Photoshop to create the digital illustrations for this book • Typography by Chelsea C. Donaldson and Caitlin Stamper • 22 23 24 25 26  RTLO  10 9 8 7 6 5 4 3 2 1 ❖ First Edition

written by **ANIKA ALDAMUY DENISE**     illustrated by **LORIS LORA**

# Phenomenal
# AOC

## THE ROOTS AND RISE OF
## ALEXANDRIA OCASIO-CORTEZ

**HARPER**

*An Imprint of HarperCollinsPublishers*

**O**N **J**ANUARY **3, 2019**,
in a white suit, the color worn by suffragettes,
gold hoops, a wink to her Bronx roots,
and red lipstick, a nod to her Latinidad,
Alexandria Ocasio-Cortez became the youngest woman
*ever* to serve in Congress.
At twenty-nine, her startling rise shocked the establishment
and shattered the status quo.

How did one young Boricua smash expectations
and become a *phenomenal force* in politics?
It begins where it *all* began—

in the Boogie Down Bronx,
home of hip-hop,
el condado de la salsa,
New York City's northern crown.

In 1989, a baby girl named Alexandria was born
in the working-class neighborhood of Parkchester,
to Sergio Ocasio and Blanca Cortez.
Her parents called her "Sandy."
Then came Gabriel, Sandy's little brother.

Life wasn't easy for Sergio and Blanca,
raising their young family while making ends meet.
But they knew the value of working
*in* and *for* your community—

Proud and resourceful,
hardworking and hopeful,
familia always came first.

When Sandy was five, her dad decided
to move the family to Yorktown Heights,
a quieter suburb with better schools,
where his children could thrive.

This was the plan.
This was the dream.
The reality?

Not everything was sunny in suburbia.
There was a divide.
Sandy saw it and felt it.

At school, her teachers sometimes discouraged her.
They didn't believe a brown girl from the BX
could be top of her class in reading, math, and science.

But Sandy proved them wrong again and again.
*Why did they underestimate her?*

The answer lay alongside the Bronx River Parkway,
as pristine houses and picket fences gave way
to bustling boulevards and brick buildings.
Traveling between two worlds,
Sandy witnessed the gaps between
wage-working and wealthy neighborhoods.

Parkchester

Yorktown wasn't better than Parkchester, but it had more *resources*.
Inequity lit a spark of activism in Sandy that would later become a fire.

Sandy's parents had scraped and saved to give her a shot, and she was *not* going to waste it.

SANDY'S COLLEGE

She enrolled premed at Boston University
and would later study abroad in Niger—
caring for expectant mothers
whose communities had been ravaged by famine.

In Sandy's second year,
she got a call no daughter wants to get.
Papi was sick.
Things had taken a bad turn.
"Make me proud" were the last words
between Sandy and Sergio.

The loss of her father
and her experience studying abroad
opened Sandy's eyes to the deep connections
between birthplace and destiny.

She switched her major to economics and international relations
and graduated with honors.

Top of her class, Sandy could have worked anywhere.
But losing Sergio had left her mother and brother struggling.

So she went back to New York—back to the Bronx—
to help and to heal.

She cleaned houses with Mami.
Then took a job as a bartender and waitress.
Working at Flats Fix was a master class
in low-wage work, immigrant labor,
and treatment of women in the workplace.
As always—Sandy was an excellent student.

She was also an activist.
Canvassing for progressive candidates,
she learned that change was made by those who organize.
By feet pounding pavement
and knuckles knocking on doors.

By *showing up* and *speaking up* for her community.

In 2016, when Sandy got the chance to go to Standing Rock Reservation
to join more than three hundred Native tribes protesting the Dakota Access Pipeline,
she saw the power of young people coming together
for climate justice and the protection of indigenous land.
At that moment, Sandy knew she could be a voice for change too.
*But how?*

Brand New Congress!

BNC needed a candidate to represent the Bronx and Queens.
Sandy's brother, Gabriel, nominated his big sister to be on the ballot.
BNC's mission?
*To make government work for all Americans.*
*All Americans, from Parkchester to Standing Rock.*

When BNC called,
Alexandria Ocasio-Cortez,
cum laude college graduate,
bartender, organizer, activist,
proud Puerto Rican daughter
from the Bronx . . .
said YES.

But like the Water Protectors protesting the pipeline—
winning would take a *grassroots* movement.
To defeat her powerful opponent, Joseph Crowley,
candidate Alexandria Ocasio-Cortez had to
build a coalition of *people,* not politicians,
of changemakers, not corporate takers,
of immigrants and dreamers
striving for justice, equity, and dignity.

So Alexandria got to work.
Door-knocking by day.
Bartending at night.
*She'll never beat him*, many thought.
Young, smart, and savvy, she used
the power of social media
to get out her message.

"*Every day gets harder for working families to get by,*"
Alexandria said. "*The rent gets higher, health care
covers less and less, and our income stays the same. . . .
We deserve a champion. It's time to fight for a
New York that working families can afford.*"

On June 26, 2018, when all the primary votes were counted,
it was Alexandria Ocasio-Cortez by a landslide.
She clobbered Crowley—a tenth-term incumbent,
heir to the powerful political machine.
"We meet a machine with a movement," said Alexandria.
That day, the phenom AOC was born.

In Washington, DC, where she would soon climb the steps of the Capitol building as the nation's youngest congresswoman—Alexandria recalled dipping her toes into the reflecting pool at the Washington Monument on a long-ago trip to the Capitol with her father.

"This is our government. It belongs to us," Sergio had told her.

Her work had just begun, but one thing was certain:
Sergio Ocasio was correct; the government of the
United States belongs to *all* people,
regardless of race, creed, wealth, or zip code.
And Alexandria had made him proud.

# "JUSTICE IS ABOUT MAKING SURE THAT BEING POLITE IS NOT THE SAME THING AS BEING QUIET. IN FACT, OFTENTIMES, THE MOST RIGHTEOUS THING YOU CAN DO IS SHAKE THE TABLE." –AOC

At just twenty-nine years old, Alexandria Ocasio-Cortez lit onto the world stage with a message and style that was fierce, bold, and direct, upending beliefs about how young women in politics—especially young women of color—should behave.

In her signature suits, red lipstick, and gold hoops, she is forever affirming who she is and where she came from. Yes, she is Boricua from the Bronx. Yes, she worked as a waitress. Yes, she is smart. Yes, she speaks truth to power. And she does it with strength and swagger.

Whether clapping back at critics on Twitter, giving cooking tutorials while explaining government policy on Instagram, or slaying the status quo on the House of Representatives floor—there's no question AOC has changed the game by bringing her unapologetic and authentic leadership to Congress.

So for all you changemakers who want to shake the table AOC style—here are five inspiring lessons straight out of the Alexandria Ocasio-Cortez playbook.

## LESSON 1: DANCE TO YOUR OWN BEAT

How do you beat bullies at their own game? Disarm them with JOY! When a social media troll tried to embarrass AOC by posting a video of her dancing in college, AOC tweeted a video of herself dancing outside her Congressional office.

*"Wait until they find out Congresswomen dance too!"* –AOC

## LESSON 2: STICK BY YOUR SQUAD

Reformistas know having friends who value and support them is *key*. Nicknamed the "Squad," the congresswomen Alexandria Ocasio-Cortez of New York, Ilhan Omar of Minnesota, Rashida Tlaib of Michigan, and Ayanna Pressley of Massachusetts—all women of color—formed a powerful sisterhood.

*"[This] friendship . . . it's not some political alliance. It's a very deep, unconditional human bond."* —AOC

## LESSON 3: KEEP CALM AND COME PREPARED

Watching Congresswoman Ocasio-Cortez work her magic on the House floor is a master class in calm, cool preparation. She does her homework and knows what to say and *how* to say it. Clips of AOC giving firebrand speeches or sharply questioning witnesses during House hearings are among the most-viewed political videos of all time.

*"People are prone to assuming that I will be not as prepared, intelligent, or good at this. . . . The good news is that being held to a higher standard forces you to meet it." —AOC*

## LESSON 4: OUR PLANET IS PRIORITY ONE

AOC understood the urgency of the climate crisis even *before* she came to Congress. Once elected, she took bold action, drafting the Green New Deal—a plan to reduce greenhouse gas emissions, build sustainable infrastructure, and create jobs.

*"The Green New Deal is the legislation of indigenous communities in the United States . . . of the residents of Flint. The Green New Deal belongs to the people of Puerto Rico . . . to the coal miners in West Virginia. It belongs to the victims of wildfires in California. And when we center our communities and allow them to lead, anything is possible." —AOC*

## LESSON 5: THE FUTURE IS YOU(TH)!

That's right, YOU! By becoming the youngest congresswoman in the United States, Alexandria Ocasio-Cortez is an electrifying example of how young people are using their power to affect global change. Kids from Boise to the Bronx are joining youth-fueled movements whose aim is a more just, equitable, and sustainable world.

*"I don't think there's any shortage of obstacles that we have ahead of us, but I don't think that we not do things just because they're hard. In fact, sometimes the hard things to do are the most worthwhile." —AOC*

## LEARN MORE ABOUT YOUTH-LED MOVEMENTS

*Climate Action*

Sunrise Movement: www.sunrisemovement.org

*Justice and Dignity for Immigrants*

United We Dream: www.unitedwedream.org

*Sensible Gun Violence Prevention*

March for Our Lives: www.marchforourlives.com

# LANGUAGE OF THE POSSIBLE

**BRAND NEW CONGRESS**: Brand New Congress recruits teachers, nurses, activists, and blue-collar workers to run for office. Their mission is to create a Congress that works for the good of all people.

**CANDIDATE**: A person who runs for election.

**CANVASSING**: To try to get support for a political candidate or issue by going door-to-door in a community to talk with voters.

**CONGRESS**: The United States Constitution divides the government into three branches: executive, legislative, and judicial. Congress is the *legislative* branch, the branch that makes laws. There are two houses of Congress: the House of Representatives and the Senate. All fifty states have members who represent them in both the House and Senate.

**CONGRESSWOMAN**: A woman who is a member of the US House of Representatives.

**DAKOTA ACCESS PIPELINE (DAPL)**: A pipeline carrying crude oil that extends across North Dakota, South Dakota, Iowa, and Illinois, crossing through communities, farms, tribal land, sensitive natural areas, and wildlife habitat. Construction of the DAPL sparked a movement led by indigenous activists called Water Protectors, who protested its violation of sacred sites and waterways.

**GRASSROOTS MOVEMENT**: A movement organized by individuals in a community rather than people in traditional positions of power.

Examples of grassroots activities are door-knocking, circulating petitions, fundraising for small donations, text messaging campaigns, and organizing demonstrations or protests.

**INCUMBENT**: In elections, *incumbent* refers to the person who is already in office and is seeking reelection.

**PRIMARY**: A preliminary election to decide who will be a party's candidate in the general election.

**PROGRESSIVE**: A person who identifies with the progressive wing of the Democratic Party. Progressives advocate for more economic and social equality and believe that government should be a tool for helping all people.

**STANDING ROCK**: The Standing Rock Sioux Reservation is situated in North and South Dakota. The people of Standing Rock, often called Sioux, are members of the Dakota and Lakota nations.

**SUFFRAGETTES**: Women who took part in the women's suffrage movement, a decades-long fight for women to win the right to vote in the United States. To signal they were a part of the movement, suffragettes dressed in white at public events.

**WAGEWORKER**: A person who works for an hourly wage, not a salary. Examples of wage-earning jobs are retail shop clerks, restaurant servers and cooks, janitors, house cleaners, and childcare providers.

## SELECTED SOURCES

Alter, Charlotte. "'Change Is Closer Than We Think.' Inside Alexandria Ocasio-Cortez's Unlikely Rise." *Time*, March 21, 2019.

Cadigan, Hillary. "Alexandria Ocasio-Cortez Learned Her Most Important Lessons from Restaurants." *Bon Appétit*, November 7, 2018.

Elizabeth, De. "Rep. Alexandria Ocasio-Cortez Speaks at 2019 Women's March in New York City." *Teen Vogue,* January 19, 2019.

Fadulu, Lola. "Alexandria Ocasio-Cortez's Next Big Effort: Tackling Poverty." *New York Times,* September 25, 2019.

Herrera, Allison. "Standing Rock activists: 'Don't call us protesters. We're water protectors.'" The World, October 31, 2016.

Read, Bridget. "36 Hours with Alexandria Ocasio-Cortez." *Vogue,* June 28, 2019.

Remnick, David. "Left Wing of the Possible." *New Yorker,* July 23, 2018.